Bright
≡**Summaries**.com

AF131390

Twelfth Night

BY WILLIAM SHAKESPEARE

BOOK ANALYSIS

By Elizabeth Smith

Twelfth Night
BY WILLIAM SHAKESPEARE

WILLIAM SHAKESPEARE

ENGLISH PLAYWRIGHT AND POET

- **Born in Stratford-upon-Avon in 1564.**
- **Died in Stratford-upon-Avon in 1616.**
- **Notable works:**
  - *Romeo and Juliet* (c. 1594), play
  - *Hamlet* (1601), play
  - *The Tempest* (1610), play

Hailed as Britain's greatest dramatist, William Shakespeare wrote and produced around 39 plays, as well as a famous sequence of 154 sonnets and two long narrative poems. He married Anne Hathaway, with whom he had three children (Susanna, Hamnet, and Judith). As well as a writer, Shakespeare was also an actor and part-owner of his playing company, the Lord Chamberlain's Men (later the King's Men). In 1599, the Lord Chamberlain's Men moved to the purpose-built Globe Theatre, which burned down in an accident involving a theatrical cannon in 1613, before being rebuilt in 1614. Besides providing a valuable insight into the Elizabethan and Jacobean times in which he lived and wrote, Shakespeare's works are often praised as timeless guides to human nature and art that continue to be relevant today.

TWELFTH NIGHT

A ROMANTIC COMEDY OF MISTAKEN IDENTITY

- **Genre:** comic play
- **Reference edition:** Shakespeare, W. (1988) *Twelfth Night*. London: Routledge, ed. Lothian, J. M. and T. W. Craik
- **1ˢᵗ edition:** written and performed c. 1601, published in the First Folio in 1623
- **Themes:** love, disguise, gender, practical jokes, madness, social class

Twelfth Night is a comic play about the romantic adventures and misadventures of the Illyrian nobles Olivia and Duke Orsino, and the identical twins Viola and Sebastian, who have been separated in a shipwreck. Viola's decision to disguise herself as a page boy called Cesario creates a love triangle which generates misunderstandings but is eventually resolved. The play's mischievous tone reflects the fact that it was probably composed for the Elizabethan festival of Twelfth Night, which was celebrated with carnivalesque reversals (servants would dress as up as their masters, for instance). The play also features the pranking and humiliation of a haughty and self-important servant called Malvolio. Under the cloak of comedy, *Twelfth Night* tackles and complicates questions of class, gender, and sexuality.

SUMMARY

ACT ONE

Duke Orsino is in love with Olivia, who is in mourning for her brother. Meanwhile, Viola has washed ashore after a shipwreck, in which she believes her brother, Sebastian, has drowned. Viola decides to go into the duke's service dressed as a boy, with the help of a captain. Sir Toby Belch is living with his niece Olivia, who is irritated by his misbehaviour, as he has brought in his foolish friend, Sir Andrew Aguecheek, as an unwanted suitor to her. Disguised as Cesario, Viola becomes a favourite page of Duke Orsino. Orsino asks Cesario/Viola to deliver his messages to Olivia. Cesario/Viola agrees, even though he/she has developed feelings for the duke. Cesario/Viola visits Olivia, who maintains she cannot love the duke, but falls for Cesario/Viola, and gives Malvolio a ring to give to him/her, claiming he/she has left it behind.

ACT TWO

Viola's brother Sebastian has survived the shipwreck with the help of his new friend, Antonio. Sebastian is the son of a dead nobleman, with a twin sister who he believes has drowned, and is going to Count Orsino's court. Antonio follows him, despite having many enemies in Orsino's court. Malvolio gives Cesario/Viola Olivia's ring. Cesario/Viola never left the ring, and figures out that Olivia has feelings for him/her. Olivia's servant Maria warns Sir Toby, Sir Andrew and the clown that Malvolio is on his way to turn them out of doors. They argue with Malvolio, but Maria has a cunning plan to make a fool of him: she will imitate Olivia's handwriting in a letter declaring her love for him. Meanwhile, Orsino discusses love with Cesario/Viola, who hints that he/she loves someone like him. Maria hides Sir Toby, Sir Andrew and Fabian (a disgruntled servant) in a hedge to wait for Malvolio, leaving a letter. Malvolio fantasises about marrying Olivia and becoming Count Malvolio. He finds the letter and falls for it. The message advises him to act surly towards the other servants, to wear yellow stockings in a cross-gartered style, and to smile as much as possible when he is with Olivia. This advice is calculated to annoy Olivia.

ACT THREE

Cesario/Viola attempts to court Olivia on Orsino's behalf, but Olivia reveals her feelings for Cesario/Viola instead, which he/she cannot return. Antonio finds Sebastian. Antonio has to keep a low profile because he is a wanted man, so they agree to meet at an inn, and he gives Sebastian his own money. Olivia summons Malvolio, who appears in his yellow stockings, grinning manically and apparently mad. Sir Toby, Fabian and Maria decide to lock him in a dark room and treat him as a madman. Sir Toby and Fabian engineer a duel between Sir Andrew and Cesario/Viola, and convince both parties that the other is a bloodthirsty opponent. Antonio appears and defends Cesario/Viola. He is then arrested on Orsino's behalf. Thinking Cesario/Viola is Sebastian, Antonio asks for his money back. Viola/Cesario denies having it, and claims not to know Antonio. Sir Toby and Sir Andrew follow her off stage to continue the fight.

ACT FOUR

Sebastian is baffled by the fact that everyone at Olivia's house seems to know him, including Sir Andrew and Sir Toby, who pick a fight with him. He is confused but pleased by Olivia's courtship of him. Maria disguises the clown as "Sir Topas the curate" to further taunt Malvolio. Sir Toby suggests they call the prank off, as he is already in trouble with Olivia. The clown gives Malvolio writing materials and agrees to give his letter to Olivia. Sebastian has been unable to find Antonio. Olivia appears with a priest and suggests that they should get married immediately, and Sebastian agrees.

ACT FIVE

The officers bring Antonio to Orsino. Cesario/Viola maintains that Antonio rescued him/her, but to Orsino, he is a "pirate". Orsino proves Cesario/Viola cannot be Sebastian because Sebastian only came into town that day, whereas Cesario/Viola has been in Orsino's service for three months. Olivia arrives, angry to see Cesario/Viola with the duke, since she believes that she has just married him. The duke threatens to kill her, then Cesario/Viola instead in a jealous rage. The priest confirms Olivia's story. Orsino tries to banish Cesario/Viola, but is interrupted by Sir Andrew calling for a surgeon for Sir Toby, because Sebastian has wounded them both, which Cesario/Viola denies. Sebastian enters apologising for the fight, and the characters realise that there are two Cesarios or Sebastians. Viola/Cesario and Sebastian each discover that the other is still alive. Orsino also benefits from this misunderstanding, if the now female Cesario/Viola truly loves him as much as he/she said he/she did. They decide to marry, but Orsino cannot see his bride as a woman because her clothes are still with the captain, and only Malvolio knows where the captain is. The clown gives Olivia Malvolio's letter, in which he explains how he has been wronged. When summoned, Malvolio produces the forged letter, and Olivia realises that Maria has orchestrated the whole plot. The conspirators admit to the prank and their motivation. We find out that Sir Toby has married Maria for writing the letter. Malvolio storms out, and Orsino sends Fabian to bring him back so they can find the captain, and he and Cesario/Viola can be married. Until then, however, he still addresses him/her as the male Cesario.

CHARACTER STUDY

VIOLA

The noble-born Viola finds herself on the shore of Illyria after surviving a shipwreck in which her twin brother has apparently drowned. She decides to make her own way by disguising herself as a young man called Cesario and joining Duke Orsino's household as a page. Orsino quickly develops a liking for her, and asks her to court Olivia on his behalf. This plan leads to confusion, however, as she falls in love with Orsino, and Olivia in turn falls for "Cesario". Viola is unable to confess her feelings for Orsino, or explain why she must reject Olivia. This ambiguity is resolved in the final scene, when Olivia marries Viola's twin brother and Orsino marries her, after it is revealed she is a woman after all.

SEBASTIAN

Viola's twin brother Sebastian is rescued from the wreck by Antonio, and is convinced that Viola has drowned. Sebastian forms a strong friendship with Antonio in the three months following the shipwreck. When he decides to investigate the town, he finds himself the subject of a case of mistaken identity due to his resemblance to Cesario, who is really Viola in disguise. Sebastian decides to go along with this strange dream, particularly since it involves marrying the beautiful Olivia.

DUKE ORSINO

The wealthy and powerful Duke Orsino is determined to win Olivia's love, despite her frequent refusals of him. As a caricature of the suffering lover, his self-indulgent lovesickness seems just as performative as Olivia's mourning. Meanwhile, he becomes increasingly attached to the handsome Cesario, a page boy who is really Viola in disguise. His attraction to Cesario adds to the play's sexual ambiguity. This ambiguity persists even in the final scene, where he continues to refer to Viola as a man in the absence of her "woman's weeds" (p. 146).

OLIVIA

The wealthy and beautiful Olivia uses her mourning for her brother as a pretext to refuse her two suitors, Duke Orsino and Sir Andrew Aguecheek, but at times her melancholy seems performative. She quickly falls for Cesario, who is really Viola in disguise, and becomes just as persistent in her affections as Orsino. In a final sleight of hand, Sebastian replaces Cesario, restoring balance to the gender ambiguity.

FESTE THE CLOWN

Like many of Shakespeare's fools, Feste is far cannier than he lets on. His influence in the play ranges from offering witty jibes and cloaked advice, to being a key player in the prank on Malvolio. Feste seems to embody the mischievous and occasionally subversive logic of the play, declaring in the final scene that the "whirligig of time" has come full circle (p. 152).

SIR TOBY BELCH

Sir Toby is living with his niece Olivia, who does not approve of his penchant for bad company, late nights and drinking. Together with his partner in crime, Maria, Sir Toby orchestrates a prank to humiliate Malvolio, who opposes the mischievous spirit the two conspirators embody.

He is so impressed by Maria's wit and ingenuity that he eventually marries her.

SIR ANDREW AGUECHEEK

Sir Andrew is friends with Sir Toby, who has strung him along with the promise of marriage to Olivia. However, Olivia is unimpressed with Sir Andrew's foolishness, which is evident to everyone except Sir Andrew himself.

MARIA

Olivia's waiting-gentlewoman is also the cunning mastermind of the prank on Malvolio, and she uses this punishment of his ambition to serve her own: she wins a favourable match to the aristocratic Sir Toby. Maria is witty and daring throughout the play, with a strong sense of mischief.

MALVOLIO

Malvolio's haughty demeanour and distaste for the spirit of fun as Sir Toby, Maria and Feste see it mark him as the principle antagonist of the play, and the target of a prank designed to expose his ambition and punish him for his self-righteousness. As well as taking himself too seriously, Malvolio's combination of ambition and self-love makes him vulnerable to the delusion that Olivia has fallen in love with him. The prank begins with Malvolio dressed ridiculously in yellow stockings, but escalates to accusations of madness and imprisonment in a dark room. Malvolio's defeat marks the victory of the mischievous spirit of the play, but also serves as an example to servants who have ideas above their station, and as such is more problematic to modern audiences.

ANTONIO

After rescuing Sebastian from the shipwreck, Antonio forms a strong attachment to him, which he describes as "love" (p. 39) with potential homoerotic implications. This devotion leads him to follow Sebastian into Illyria, despite being wanted on pain of death for piracy. Confusing Cesario for Sebastian, Antonio defends him in a duel, before being arrested. Cesario has no knowledge of him or the money he gave to Sebastian, and Antonio believes he has been betrayed until the revelation of the two Sebastians in the final scene.

ANALYSIS

MISTAKEN IDENTITY AND SEXUAL AMBIGUITY

The disguise at the root of *Twelfth Night*'s misunderstandings, that of Viola, results in her becoming embroiled in a love triangle, whilst freeing her from the gender expectations that would normally confine her to a more passive role. When she is dressed as a man, it becomes socially acceptable for Viola to seek her fortune. Disguised as Cesario, she is indistinguishable from Sebastian, a fact which hints at the arbitrary nature of the distinction between sexes. However, the plot can only be resolved by her return to a traditional female role. Viola's appearance as Cesario is also a source of sexual ambiguity, creating what is in effect two same-sex relationships (Olivia is attracted to Viola as Cesario, and feelings grow between Orsino and Cesario/Viola). The carnivalesque atmosphere of the comedy creates a space for exploring same-sex desire in a culture otherwise hostile to it.

Antonio is prepared to risk arrest and death for Sebastian, whom he "adore[s]" (p. 40), a sentiment which may suggest homosexual attraction on his part. *Twelfth Night*, like many of Shakespeare's comedies, concludes with a return to order and conformity, and as such Antonio's love is left out of the equation in favour of more traditional heterosexual relationships.

Just as these relationships are called into question, however, by the ambiguity that has preceded them, the stability of identity is undermined by the use of disguise. This instability further extends to the theatre itself. Viola statement that "I am not what I am" (p. 82) applies not only to her disguise as Cesario, but also to the Renaissance actor behind the character. When *Twelfth Night* was first performed, women were banned from the stage, so both identity and gender were further blurred by the fact that Viola was probably played by a boy actor. In this carnivalesque blurring of disguises and genders, identity becomes a series of performances, rather than a single stable "self". When Sebastian and Cesario/Viola appear onstage together, an astonished Antonio asks "how have you made division of yourself?" (p. 143) A fear that disguise leads to self-division and the erosion of a stable self haunts the many plays about disguise across Shakespeare's canon, and Jacobean theatre as a whole. One identity does not displace another, hence Viola remains dressed as Cesario in the final scene, and Orsino continues to call him/ her "Cesario", "[f]or so you shall be while you are a man" (p. 153). The gender reversals of *Twelfth Night* therefore reflect a Renaissance anxiety about the performativity of identity.

LOVE AND INCONSTANCY

Orsino's unrequited passion for Olivia fits a popular Jacobean model of heterosexual love, that of the archetypal unrequited lover of contemporary courtly poetry. The duke even claims that "such as I am, all lovers be", and his passion is universal enough to be caricatured (p. 56). His performance as suffering lover makes Orsino's supposedly deep passion seem superficial, particularly considering how quickly he transfers his affections from the newly married Olivia to the newly discovered Viola. The fool draws attention to this inconstancy when he calls Orsino's mind "a very opal" (p. 60) (as the opal is considered to be a changeable gemstone). Likewise, if Olivia is just as happy with one twin as with the other, her love seems to be based largely on appearances. Antonio's sexually ambiguous love is constant in comparison, but ultimately unfulfilled. Viola's unwavering devotion to Orsino goes against the gender stereotype of the fickle woman, and ironically disproves Orsino's own assertions that no woman could love as deeply as him. In a play characterised by uncertainty and reversal, the stability of love is inevitably called into question.

A JOKE TAKEN TOO FAR

Shakespeare uses the prank on Malvolio to test the boundaries of the genre of comedy. Tricking Malvolio into wearing yellow stockings is as harmless as it is amusing. However, the prank quickly escalates into imprisonment in a dark room, and can strike modern audiences as going too far, to the point that even Sir Toby feels uncomfortable. Somewhere along the way, Malvolio's suffering crosses the line from humorous to disquieting. The undercurrent of class prejudice underlying the prank can also make us uncomfortable, though it probably had a different effect on Shakespeare's audience. In Jacobean England, previously rigid class boundaries were beginning to allow for more movement, leading to fears about the erosion of social structures. As an ambitious servant who reaches above his station, Malvolio is the perfect scapegoat for these anxieties, and his humiliation releases tension for the audience as well as the pranksters onstage. When it comes to exploring gender and sexuality, the humour of *Twelfth Night* removes inhibitions and subverts boundaries. In the case of Malvolio, however, comedy can also entrench boundaries. In this light, Maria's role in the prank is somewhat ironic. Ambitious and enterprising, Maria uses the humiliation of an over-reaching servant to raise her own social status by marrying Sir Toby. Despite Olivia's judgement that Malvolio has been "notoriously abus'd" (p. 152), and the confession of the pranksters, the play finishes abruptly before the characters can punish or applaud them. Malvolio's own premature exit and vague promise of revenge leaves this question undecided. Whether the "sportful malice" (p. 151) of the prank is deserving of "laughter" or "revenge" is therefore left up to the audience.

A HAPPY ENDING?

One of the key characteristics of a comic play is a neat ending, in which couples are happily married off. On the surface, *Twelfth Night* is resolved in such a way, with the marriage of Sebastian and Olivia, and the impeding wedding of Orsino and Viola. However, on closer inspection, none of the characters marry the person they originally wanted. After Olivia marries somebody else, Orsino rapidly transfers his affections to Viola, who he sees at least partially as Cesario. Olivia fell in love with Viola as Cesario, who is replaced by Sebastian without Olivia's knowledge. Antonio's love is unfulfilled, and he has no further lines after expressing his surprise at Sebastian's division. In many other ways, the apparently concrete conclusion of the play is actually open-ended. The captain is never located, and as a result Viola never returns to herself. Not only is she dressed as Cesario as the play ends, but Orsino appears to still think of her as her male persona. Malvolio exits the stage before he can lead the characters to Viola's clothes or bring about a conclusion to the prank sequence, instead deferring it with threats of revenge. Despite the coupling off of four of the characters and the ostensible return to order, the clown has the last word, as a representative of the carnivalesque atmosphere of the Twelfth Night festivities.

FURTHER REFLECTION

SOME QUESTIONS TO THINK ABOUT...

- What impact do clothes have on identity in the play? Think about Viola's "woman's weeds" (p. 146) and Malvolio's yellow stockings.
- Malvolio and Maria both share a similar ambition to better themselves. Why is Maria's ambition seen as being more acceptable, while Malvolio is condemned for his?
- Is the play's ending satisfying? Explain your answer.
- "If music be the food of love, play on" (p. 5). What is the role of music in *Twelfth Night*?
- In Act Four, Scene One, Sebastian asks "are all the people mad?" (p. 118) Who exactly is mad: a single character, none of the characters, or the entire play?
- Can love be constant where identity is in flux?
- "And thus the whirligig of time brings in his revenges" (p. 152). Do you agree with Feste that the prank on Malvolio delivers a kind

of justice for his attitude towards the other characters?

- What are the main differences in how audiences during Shakespeare's time might have responded to the play, compared with modern ones?

We want to hear from you!
Leave a comment on your online library
and share your favourite books on social media!

FURTHER READING

REFERENCE EDITION

- Shakespeare, W. (1988) *Twelfth Night*. London: Routledge, ed. Lothian, J. M. and T. W. Craik.

REFERENCE STUDIES

- Callaghan, D. ed. (2001) *A Feminist Companion to Shakespeare*. London: Wiley & Sons.
- Greenblatt, S. (1980) *Renaissance Self-Fashioning: From More to Shakespeare*. Chicago: University of Chicago Press.

ADAPTATIONS

- *She's The Man*. (2006) [Film]. Andy Finkman. Dir. United States: Lakeshore Entertainment, The Donners' Company, DreamWorks Pictures.
- *Twelfth Night or What you Will*. (1996) [Film]. Trevor Nunn. Dir. United Kingdom: BBC Films, Summit Entertainment.

MORE FROM BRIGHTSUMMARIES.COM

- Reading guide – *A Midsummer Night's Dream* by William Shakespeare.

- Reading guide – *Hamlet* by William Shakespeare.

- Reading guide – *Macbeth* by William Shakespeare.

- Reading guide – *Othello* by William Shakespeare.

- Reading guide – *Romeo and Juliet* by William Shakespeare.

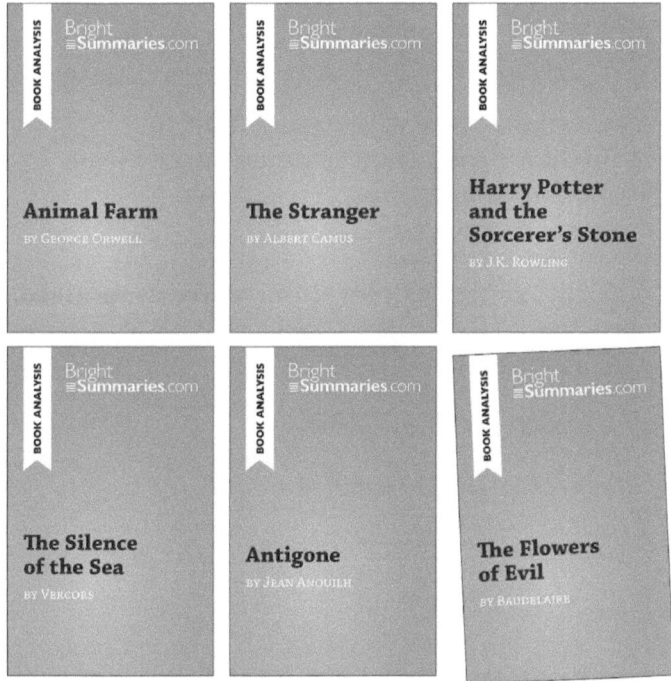

www.brightsummaries.com

Ebook EAN: 9782808012409

Paperback EAN: 9782808012416

Legal Deposit: D/2018/12603/375

Cover: © Primento

Digital conception by Primento, the digital partner of
publishers.